peanut

Written and illustrated by Lindsay Nolan

peanut

A storybook for mighty preemie babies

Written and illustrated by Lindsay Nolan

Copyright ©2015 Lindsay Nolan

Published by Lindsay Nolan
Omaha, Nebraska

Gratitude is extended to NICU doctors and nurses, whose work is appreciated beyond expressed words.

Printed in the United States of America

First Printing, 2015

ISBN: 978-0-578-16920-0

For my own miracle baby, Henry.

To her Peanut, Mama said,
"Straight to you, my heart led,
remember this, it goes unsaid...
I love everything about you."

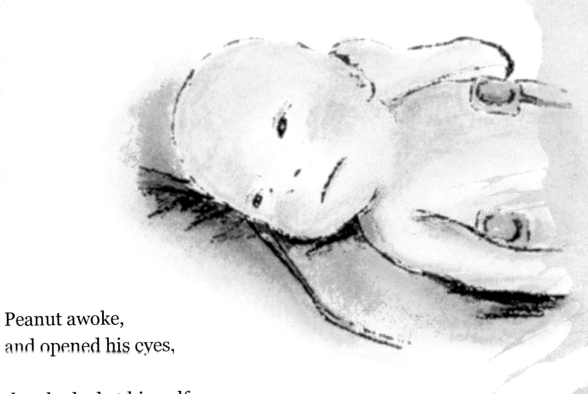

Peanut awoke,
and opened his eyes,

then looked at himself
and noticed his size;

he knew he was smaller,
and wished he was taller...

he was littler than most peanuts he knew.

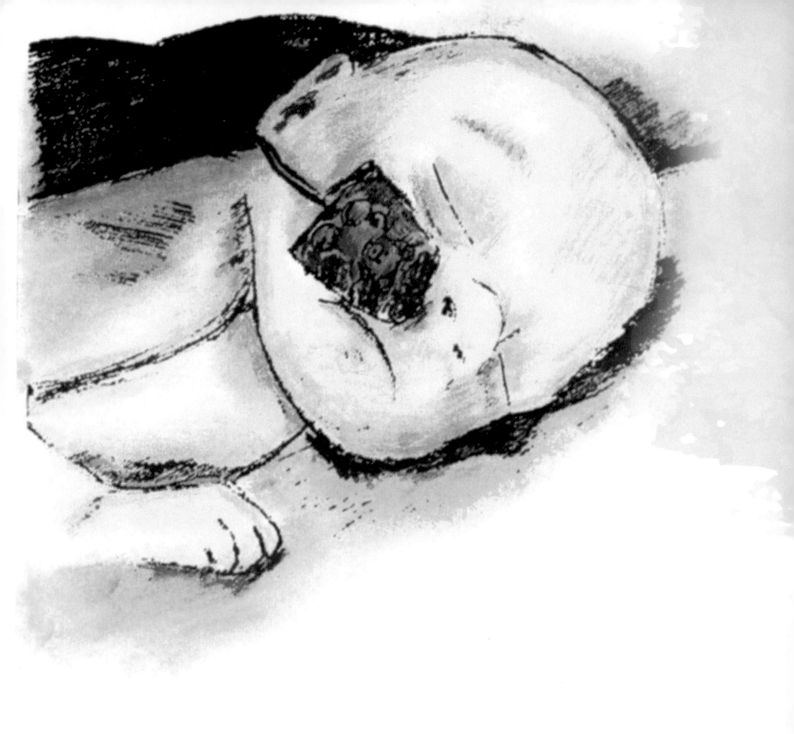

To her Peanut, Mama said,
"My preemie seed, you've been misled,
my love exceeds the length you spread...
I love everything about you."

Little Peanut,
grew and grew,

a mighty peanut
through and through,

he had to be tougher,
as life was much rougher...

for him more than most peanuts he knew.

To her Peanut, Mama said,
"In the NICU is my bed,
prayers focused on what's ahead...
I love everything about you."

Day after day,
Peanut did grow,
and Mama did show
her love for her baby.

Night after night,
Peanut did sleep,
and Mama did keep
her love for her baby.

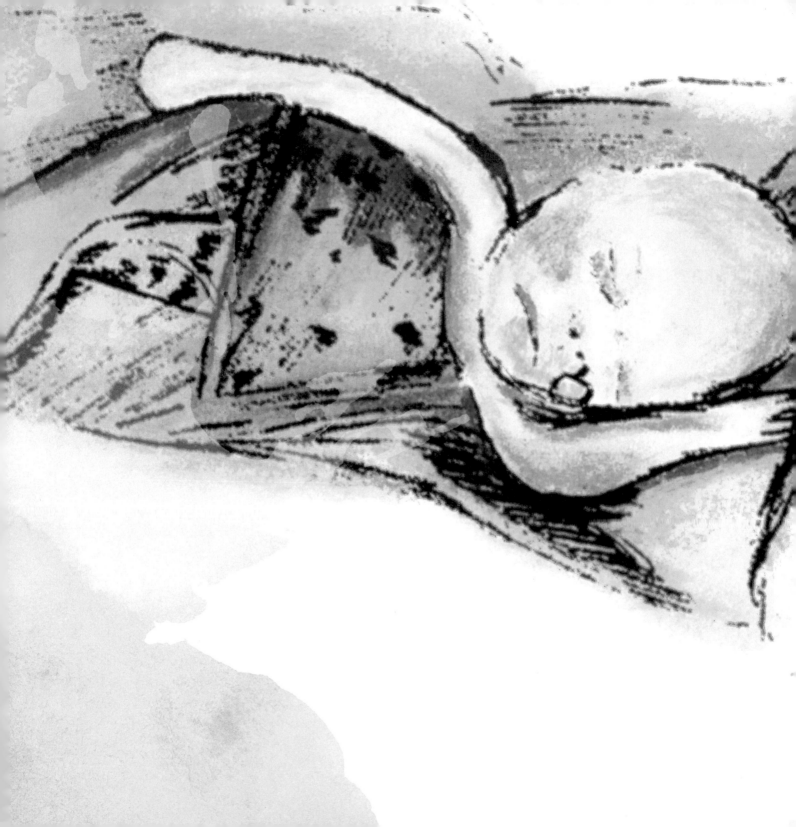

Peanut awoke,
and opened his eyes,

then looked at himself
and noticed his size;

He knew he was taller,
when once he was smaller...

he was mightier than most peanuts he knew.

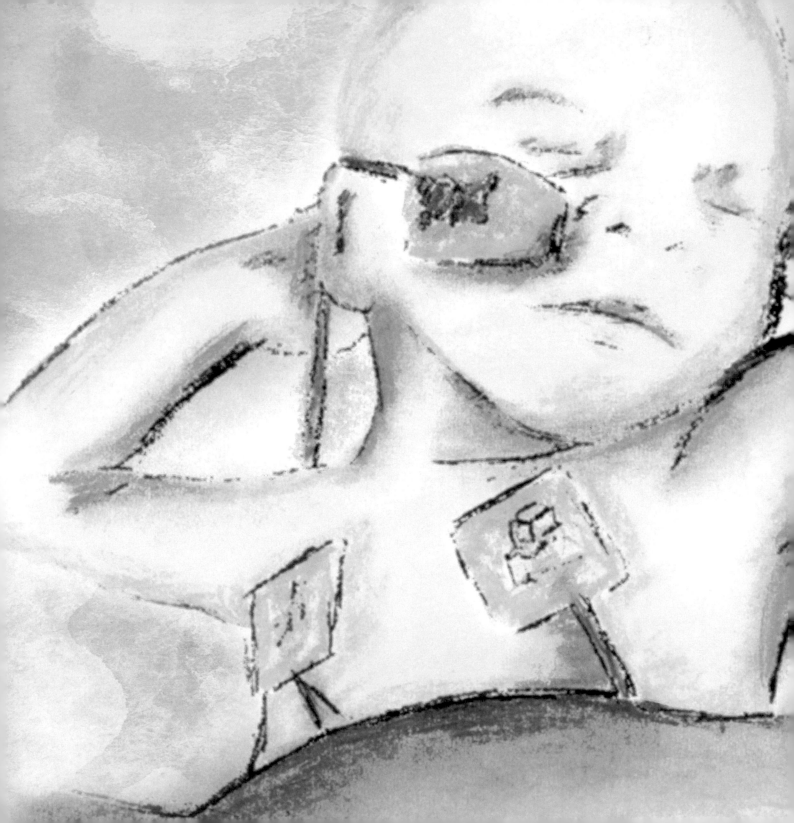

To her Peanut, Mama said,
"My wish for you is to embed
my faith in God,
my daily bread;"
Looking at Peanut, as she pled:

"Little baby,
I understand
that life never goes
exactly as planned,

and that something so little
can be something so grand.

My plans may have changed but
remaining at hand,

forever, my baby,
my heart will expand...

I love everything about you."

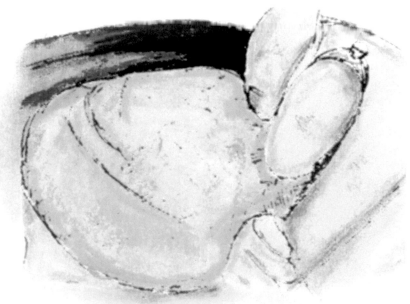

Thank you to neonatal intensive care unit doctors and nurses who work day and night to keep our babies safe and healthy. –LN

Made in the USA
Middletown, DE
03 March 2019